SOCIAL MEDIA
MADE ME
do it

SOCIAL MEDIA MADE ME do it

WALLO267

NANNY'S HOUSE PUBLISHING

Pennsauken, New Jersey

Cover Design: Kamera Krew LLC
Interior Design: Jessica Angerstein
Mananging Company: IV MGMT, LLC

Cataloging-in-Publication Data is on file with the Library of Congress.

Paperback ISBN: 979-8-9945002-0-0
ebook ISBN: 979-8-9945002-1-7
Audio book ISBN: 979-8-9945002-2-4

1 2 3 4 5 6 7 8 9 10
First edition, January 2026

This book is dedicated to everyone who lost themselves chasing validation, numbers, and opinions that never loved them back.

To those who confused attention for affirmation and applause for acceptance.

May these pages help you take your power back, reclaim your identity, and remember who you were before the algorithm started shaping your decisions.

Contents

Introduction | How Attention Became the Most
Dangerous Drug 1

1 | Social Media Made Me Do It.. 9

2 | The First Like is the First Hit 17

3 | Before the Internet There Was the Need 25

4 | When Going Viral Rewrites Identity............................. 31

5 | Turning Pain Into Performance 39

6 | Why Anger Always Wins.. 47

7 | Clout Over Character.. 55

8 | Love as Leverage 63

9 | The Fear Economy... 71

10 | When Validation Becomes Identity............................... 79

11 | Algorithms Do Not Care About You............................. 87

12 | The Pressure to Stay Relevant 95

13 | Comparison Is the Quiet Killer..................................... 101

14 | The Crash After the Applause....................................... 109

15 | Social Media Did Not Change You, It Revealed You... 117

16 | Being Seen Without Being Consumed 123

17 | Who Are You Without Witnesses................................. 131

18 | Using Social Media Instead of Needing It 137

19 | Attention is Not Love 143

About the Author 149

Intro | How Attention Became the Most Dangerous Drug

There was a time when attention was incidental.

You lived your life, and occasionally someone noticed. You worked, struggled, built relationships, made mistakes, and attention showed up as a byproduct of proximity. People saw you because they were near you. Feedback came from faces, not numbers. Validation came slowly, inconsistently, and usually from people who knew enough about you to hold you accountable.

That world no longer exists.

Today, attention is instant.

Unlimited.

Quantified.

And detached from responsibility.

You no longer need to be in proximity to be seen. You no longer need a relationship to be validated. You no longer need consistency to be recognized. You only need impact. And impact does not care whether it comes from truth, pain, outrage, or distortion.

That shift changed people-not all at once, not dramatically, but quietly, over time.

This book exists because something subtle but dangerous happened when attention became cheap and abundant. Attention stopped being a feedback loop; it became something you could receive at will instead of something that emerged naturally from interacting with others.

And when attention is unlimited, behavior changes.

People are not addicted to social media. That framing is too simple and too forgiving. People are addicted to what attention does to their nervous systems. They are addicted to the relief that arrives when someone reacts to them. To the feeling that something they did landed somewhere outside their own mind.

Strangely, that feeling does not register as happiness. It registers as relief: relief from invisibility, from insignificance, from the quiet fear that if no one responds, maybe you do not matter.

Most people never admit to that fear. Many don't even consciously recognize it. But the body recognizes it immediately. And when attention interrupts that discomfort, the body learns fast.

This is where the danger begins.

For most of human history, identity was reinforced offline. Through family roles. Through work. Through contribution. Through consequence. You knew who you were because your life pushed back. People responded to you in real time. You felt the weight of your actions because reaction was unavoidable.

Now identity is negotiated publicly. It's tested in comments, adjusted based on engagement, and reinforced or rejected by numbers that refresh every second.

And when attention becomes the primary form of feedback, people stop asking whether something is true, aligned, or healthy. They start asking whether or not it performs.

Performance becomes protection.

This book is not a condemnation of social media platforms. Platforms are tools. They do what tools are designed to do. They amplify. They reward engagement. They surface what holds attention. Expecting morality from an algorithm is a misunderstanding of how systems work.

The real story is human.

This book is about what happens when unmet emotional needs collide with unlimited amplification.

Social media did not invent insecurity. It did not invent loneliness. It did not invent the desire to be chosen. Those longings existed long before WiFi. What changed is how fast relief can arrive now. And how public the exchange has become. How very little internal grounding is required before external validation shows up.

A single post can outperform a decade of lived experience. A moment of reaction can eclipse years of quiet growth. That imbalance matters.

When attention arrives faster than identity can form, people begin confusing visibility with worth. They mistake reaction for connection. They believe being watched is the same as being known.

It is not. Being known requires time. Being watched only requires spectacle.

This is why people say things they never thought they would say. Share things they never intended to share. Cross boundaries they once believed were firm. And when the aftermath feels heavier than expected, when the behavior no longer aligns with their self-image, a ready explanation is waiting.

Social media made me do it.

That sentence sounds harmless. Casual. Almost humorous. But underneath it is a quiet surrender of agency. A decision to blame a system rather than confront a need.

Social media did not force anyone to behave out of character. It removed the friction that once slowed behavior down. It eliminated pauses. It shortened reflection. It allowed impulse to travel farther than intention.

Before, shame had weight, reputation lingered, and attention required effort.

Now, a moment of impulse can be broadcast globally before understanding even arrives. And once it is out there, it becomes permanent, not because it was meaningful, but because it was noticed.

This book is about what happens when being noticed becomes more important than being whole.

Being whole requires patience, but being noticed requires speed.

People adjust without realizing they are adjusting. They learn what gets ignored and what gets rewarded. They learn which version of themselves gets reactions and which disappears. Over time, they stop trusting their quiet instincts and start calibrating themselves to external response.

This is not vanity. It is conditioning.

When attention becomes a regulator instead of a byproduct, the nervous system adapts. Silence begins to feel uncomfortable. Stillness feels like disappearance and privacy feels like erasure.

People say they feel off when they do not post. Empty. Restless. Unsettled. They call it boredom or burnout, but underneath it is something else.

Withdrawal.

They are deprived of the thing that has been quietly calming them.

This is why telling people to log off rarely works. You cannot remove a regulator without understanding what it replaced.

Attention has replaced things it was never meant to replace: belonging, identity, and self-trust.

This book is not here to shame anyone for wanting attention. Wanting to be seen is human. Wanting to be heard is human. Wanting to matter is human. What is dangerous is pretending that attention is harmless simply because it is common.

The most dangerous things rarely arrive as extremes; they arrive normalized. They are justified casually. And repeated daily.

This book is for people who feel that shift.

It's for creators who feel hollow after posting, for people who have gone viral and felt smaller afterward, and for anyone who has shared something publicly and immediately wondered why.

It is also for people who insist they are unaffected. Those who believe they are simply using the tools. Those who believe they are in control.

Influence does not require belief. It requires exposure.

The goal of this book is not to offer a detox, not to provide a program, not to tell anyone what to do. The goal is awareness. Because awareness restores agency.

Once you understand what attention is doing to your behavior, you can no longer pretend it is accidental. You can stop outsourcing responsibility to systems. And you can start asking better questions.

Who am I when no one is watching? What do I value when it is not rewarded? What parts of me only exist online? What parts disappear when the phone is down?

These questions are uncomfortable. They should be. Growth does not begin with comfort. It begins with clarity.

Attention did not become dangerous because it exists. It became dangerous because it replaced things that require *depth*.

This book is an invitation to look honestly at that trade. To examine not with shame, not with blame, but with responsibility.

Because social media did not make anyone do anything.

It simply made it easier to avoid noticing who we are becoming. Once you notice that, you cannot unsee it.

And that is where this book truly begins.

1 | Social Media Made Me Do It

People say it like it explains everything.

Social media made me do it.

They say it casually. Almost joking. Sometimes defensive. Sometimes relieved. As if the sentence itself closes the case. As if now the behavior belongs to the platform, not to them. As if responsibility slipped the moment the screen lit up.

That sentence has become the most socially accepted excuse of our time.

It's the phrase people reach for when they feel uncomfortable standing in what they did. When a choice looks uglier in hindsight than it felt in the moment. When behavior doesn't match the identity they believe they have.

Because if social media made you do it, then you didn't really choose it.

You were influenced, pulled in, caught up.

That framing feels safer than saying, I wanted the reaction more than I wanted the restraint.

But social media has never forced anyone to do anything.

It didn't force people to lie about their lives. It didn't force people to publicly embarrass themselves. It didn't force people to expose private moments, monetize their pain, or sacrifice dignity for engagement.

What it did was remove the pause.

Before attention lived online, behavior had friction. You had to sit with your thoughts longer before acting. You had to read the room. You had to look people in the eye. You had to feel the temperature shift when you crossed a line. The consequences arrived immediately because the witnesses were human and right in front of you.

Social media changed the environment.

It created a space where behavior could be broadcast without proximity. Where a reaction could arrive without a relationship, and where feedback could come without context. Individual faces were replaced by numbers, and accountability was replaced by engagement metrics.

And when that happened, performance became safer than honesty.

People do things online that they would never do in a room full of people they respect. Not because they are braver, but because the room feels almost imaginary. The audience feels abstract, and the damage feels delayed.

That delay is where responsibility starts slipping.

When people say it's *just content*, what they really mean is *I don't want to sit with the cost*. Calling something content makes it feel strategic rather than impulsive. Content becomes a shield.

It allows people to explain behavior without explaining themselves. It creates distance between who someone is and what they're willing to do for attention.

"I was just joking."

"It's not that serious."

"That's what people like."

These aren't explanations; they're anesthetics. They numb the discomfort of recognizing yourself in a moment you don't like.

At some point, behavior stopped being behavior and started being performance. Pain became content. Confession became branding. Outrage became currency.

And the most dangerous part is that it didn't feel like selling out. It felt like adapting! Like survival. It felt natural and like keeping up with the rules of a game everyone else was already playing.

We didn't know it at the time, but attention slowly replaced self-trust. Self-trust became something people outsourced to reactions they could quantify.

When someone says *social media made me do it,* what they're really saying is *I didn't feel real until someone reacted.*

That reaction doesn't feel like joy in the moment; it feels like relief. Like exhaling after holding your breath longer than you realized. Like proof that you registered—and mattered—somewhere outside your own head.

For people who grew up unseen, that feeling is powerful.

Social media didn't invent insecurity or loneliness. It didn't invent the desire to be chosen. Those longings existed long before screens. What changed is how fast the relief arrives now. How public the exchange has become. How little internal grounding is required before external validation shows up.

Post something vulnerable, shocking, or reckless, and watch the awareness metrics grow.

When the numbers grow, it feels like validation, even when the content costs you something. Even when it costs privacy. Even when it costs relationships. Some things you can't get back once the clip circulates.

Where does that responsibility lie?

Because if the platform made you do it, you never have to ask why you wanted the reaction so badly. You never have to confront the hunger underneath the post. You never have to acknowledge the part of you that needed witnesses more than wisdom.

Social media didn't create that hunger; it only relieved it.

Every post begins before the post. There is always a moment before the moment. A quiet decision where someone trades something internal for something external. Sometimes the trade feels harmless. Sometimes it feels necessary. It may begin to feel automatic.

But it is still a choice.

The danger isn't that people post too much. The danger is that people explain away who they become when they do. When behavior becomes performance, authenticity becomes optional. Integrity becomes flexible, and identity becomes adjustable.

People start calibrating themselves to what works. They learn what provokes reaction and what disappears. And slowly, without realizing it, they stop asking whether something is aligned. They only ask whether it performs.

That is why *social media made me do it* sounds believable. It creates distance between the person and the act. It reframes agency as pressure. It turns responsibility into circumstance.

But pressure doesn't erase choice. It reveals priorities.

This book isn't here to shame anyone for wanting attention. Wanting to be seen is human. Wanting to be heard is human. Wanting connection and a sense of belonging is human.

What isn't harmless is pretending the screen is the reason you crossed lines you were already curious about.

Social media didn't make you lie. It didn't make you overshare. It didn't make you chase reactions over respect.

It gave you permission to stop asking yourself why.

That's why people wake up confused by their own actions. That's why they say or do things they never imagined. That's why they become someone they barely recognize.

Social media made me do it.

But nothing that costs you your self-respect happens without participation. The screen didn't steal your agency. It just made it easier to avoid it.

This book starts here because accountability does *not* begin with judgment. It begins with honesty. And sometimes honesty requires saying something uncomfortable.

Social media *didn't* make you do it.

It made it easier not to notice who you were becoming. It made it easier for performance to replace identity.

That is the real danger.

This is where the story begins.

2 | The First Like Is the First Hit

The first like does not feel exciting.

It feels relieving.

That distinction matters more than most people understand.

Excitement is sharp. It spikes and fades. Relief settles deeper. It loosens something tight in the chest. It quiets a background tension that has been running for a long time before the post ever went live. When the first reaction appears, the body does not celebrate. It exhales.

Because before the reaction, there is uncertainty, a subtle unease, a quiet question that sits beneath the act of posting: *Will this matter? Will anyone respond? Will I disappear here?*

When the first like appears, it interrupts that discomfort. The brain now registers connection. The nervous system registers safety. Not happiness. Not fulfillment. Safety.

That is why the first like stays with people. It is not about numbers; it is about regulation.

Inside the brain, a simple learning loop begins to form. A chemical reward is released, driven by dopamine. Dopamine is often misunderstood as the happiness chemical. It is not. Dopamine is the anticipation chemical. It motivates pursuit. It trains the brain to repeat behaviors that reduce discomfort or increase reward.

Dopamine does not say *This feels good*. It says *Do this again*. That is the danger.

The brain learns fast: a post triggers a reaction, and reaction leads to relief.

And once that connection is formed, it does not need conscious intention to repeat. The body remembers before the mind does.

This is why people do not stop after one post. It is not vanity. It is not an obsession. It is conditioning. The first like becomes a reference point. Every post that follows is measured against it. Not logically. Physiologically.

Did it hit the same? Did it land the same? Did it calm the same?

When the answer is no, the discomfort returns. It's a subtle restlessness at first. A need to refresh and check again, or to adjust if needed.

People begin tweaking the variables: the caption, the timing, the tone.

They call it strategy. They call it optimization. But underneath it is a body trying to recreate a feeling it remembers and craves.

Rarely do people ask the deeper question: *Why did this reaction matter so much to me?*

Because the answer is uncomfortable. It is uncomfortable to admit that something external regulates what something internal cannot.

Social media accelerates this process by removing the delay of long term feedback. There is no waiting period. No slow reinforcement of identity. The loop is instant: Post. Refresh. React.

Speed matters.

When relief arrives quickly, the nervous system does not learn patience. It learns dependency. The faster the reward, the stronger the habit.

This is how attention addiction forms without anyone ever deciding to be addicted. People are not logging on to feel important. They are logging on to feel settled. To quiet the unease. To confirm that they still register.

But over time, tolerance builds, and the reference point moves.

What once felt validating is now starting to feel normal. What once felt exciting becomes baseline. The body needs more stimulation to achieve the same relief.

This is where escalation begins.

People share more, reveal more, *perform* more.

Not because they are chasing fame, but because the original dose no longer works.

The first post might be honest. Safe. Relatively contained. The reaction feels good. Encouraging. Reassuring.

The next post goes further, then further still–not intentionally, but automatically.

The system teaches a simple lesson: This version of you gets a response.

When expectation replaces gratitude, the dynamic shifts. Attention is no longer a bonus. It becomes a requirement. And requirements create pressure.

That pressure shows up quietly. People check metrics reflexively. They monitor reactions. They feel a small spike of anxiety when engagement dips and a small wave of relief when it rises.

This is not ego. It is nervous system conditioning. If its reaction calms you, its absence unsettles you.

Silence stops feeling neutral. It feels like an absence. Like something is missing. Like proof that something about you did not land.

This is why people say they feel off when they do not post. Empty. Restless. Disconnected. They call it boredom or burnout, but underneath it is something else.

Withdrawal.

They are deprived of the thing that has been quietly regulating them. This is where people confuse validation with joy.

Joy is steady. Validation is conditional. Joy comes from alignment. Validation comes from response. And validation is easier.

The internet does not tell people they are worthy. It tells them they are interesting. Those are not the same thing. Interest fades quickly. Worth stabilizes.

When someone confuses the two, they chase interest, hoping it will eventually settle into worth.

But it never does; it escalates instead. The escalation is not a moral failure. It is chemical learning layered onto emotional need.

Once the loop is formed, it runs in the background. People post without knowing why, scroll without intention, and share without processing.

The body leads. The mind rationalizes.

This is why telling people to just stop posting rarely works. You cannot remove a regulator without replacing it. The body will resist.

The first like taught the nervous system something simple: *This feels good.*

The brain did not ask whether it was healthy. It asked whether it worked.

And it did.

That is why the chase begins.

Not because people are shallow, but because relief feels necessary. Understanding this matters. Without it, the behavior appears to be vanity. With it, the behavior reveals conditioning.

The first like is not the problem. It is the moment the body learns where comfort comes from. Once that lesson is learned, attention becomes non-negotiable. It becomes medicine.

Medicine taken without dosage control always turns into dependency. That is the part people underestimate: not the post, not the platform, but the relief.

Because once relief is externalized, the self loses its ability to regulate without witnesses.

And that is where attention becomes dangerous.

Not because it exists, but because it starts replacing something it was never meant to replace.

3 | Before the Internet There Was the Need

The hunger for attention did not begin online.

It existed long before timelines and feeds. Long before likes and comments. Long before anyone could quantify being seen. Social media did not invent the need. It simply found it waiting.

Many people grew up learning that attention was not guaranteed. That presence did not always mean connection. Being in the room did not ensure being acknowledged. Some were raised in homes where emotions were minimized. Others in environments where praise was inconsistent or conditional. Some were surrounded by people and still felt alone.

They were not necessarily abused. They were overlooked.

That distinction matters.

Being unseen does not always come from trauma. Sometimes it comes from distraction. From emotionally unavailable caregivers. From environments where survival mattered more than attunement. From families where love existed but attention was scarce.

Children adapt to that absence quietly. Some become loud. Some become invisible. Some become excellent. Some become agreeable.

But all of them learn the same underlying lesson. Attention equals safety.

When a child is consistently mirrored, they develop a sense of internal confirmation. They learn who they are because someone reflected them back with care. When that mirroring is missing, identity becomes fragile. Self trust struggles to form.

Those children often grow into adults who look outward for confirmation. Not because they are weak, but because the internal structure was never reinforced.

Social media did not create that pattern. It rewarded it.

For someone who spent years feeling unseen, being noticed later does not feel indulgent. It feels corrective. Like something delayed. Like a missing piece finally arriving.

That is why attention lands differently for different people.

For one person, a like is pleasant. For another, it is grounding. The difference is history.

When attention finally arrives for someone who has been deprived of it, the nervous system does not register it as novelty. It registers it as relief. As stabilization. As proof that something was wrong before and is right now.

Social media delivers that relief instantly.

Instead of slowly building identity through experience, people can receive confirmation in seconds. Instead of earning belonging through consistency, they can borrow it through reaction.

Borrowed belonging never settles. It has to be renewed.

This is why some people feel anxious when they do not post. Why silence feels heavy. Why absence feels like disappearance. It is not about vanity. It is about regulation.

Attention calms what emotional absence destabilizes.

When attention becomes the regulator, people instinctively protect access to it.

That is when behavior begins to escalate.

It rarely starts extreme. The first post is often careful, honest, and measured. The response feels affirming, encouraging, and safe.

The body remembers. The next post goes a little further. Then further still.

Not because the person is manipulative, but because they are responsive. They learn what gets noticed. And what gets noticed begins to shape who they are allowed to be.

This is where identity starts bending.

People begin editing themselves to match the response. They adjust tone, story, and expression. Gradually. Not consciously. They are not lying. They are curating.

Over time, the question shifts: It is no longer *Who am I?* It becomes *Who gets reacted to?*

That shift fractures identity.

The private self and the public self begin drifting apart. The person becomes someone online that they cannot sustain offline. And that gap feels like emptiness.

Social media did not cause that emptiness. It exposed it.

For people whose early relationships lacked consistency, online validation feels familiar. You perform. You receive. You adjust. You repeat.

It mirrors the original pattern.

Familiar pain feels safer than unfamiliar health.

This is why oversharing feels natural to some people. Why boundaries feel uncomfortable. Why exposure feels like connection.

They are not seeking sympathy. They are seeking regulation.

They are trying to stabilize something internal using something external.

The internet becomes a stand-in for what was missing.

Validation replaces reassurance. Engagement replaces attunement. Numbers replace nurture.

Because the feedback is immediate. The relief feels real. But it does not heal. Attention does not resolve neglect; it distracts from it. The unseen child becomes a visible adult without becoming grounded.

Visibility without grounding is dangerous.

It makes people malleable. It makes identity negotiable. It teaches people to abandon parts of themselves that do not perform.

This is why telling people to log off misses the point. The hunger follows them offline if it is not addressed internally.

People do not crave attention because they are empty. They crave it because something meaningful was absent long enough that attention feels like repair.

This book does not judge that. It names it.

Because without naming it, people keep blaming platforms for patterns that started long before the first post.

Social media did not create the need to be seen. It monetized it. And for people who never learned how to see themselves without witnesses, that monetization becomes a trap. Not because it is pleasurable, but because it is familiar.

That familiarity is what gives attention its power.

It feels like home even when it is harming you.

And until that origin is understood, everything that follows appears to be bad behavior rather than an unmet need.

This chapter matters because it explains the why beneath the what.

Without it, people keep asking how to stop posting. With it, they begin asking a harder question: *What am I trying to regulate with attention?*

That question does not come with quick answers.

But it is the first honest one.

4 | When Going Viral Rewrites Identity

Going viral feels like winning.

That is how it is framed. That is how it is celebrated. That is how it is remembered. A sudden surge of attention. A spike in numbers. A moment where the internet agrees, loudly and all at once, that you matter.

But going viral is not just an event.

It is an interruption. It disrupts how you see yourself, how others see you, and, most dangerously, how your worth is measured.

For many people, one viral moment outperforms their entire real life. Years of effort, growth, discipline, and complexity get eclipsed by a single clip, post, or sentence. The internet does not see the full person. It sees the version that landed.

And once that happens, the rules change.

Before, identity was something you carried privately. It was reinforced by consistency, by people who know you in different moods, by effort that compounds quietly. After virality, identity became something the audience hands back to you.

You are no longer who you were. You are who they reacted to.

That shift is subtle at first. It feels flattering. Affirming. Like recognition finally arrived. People repeat your words back to you. They quote you. They tag you. They expect you to keep showing up as the version that made them feel something.

Expectation is the real cost of virality.

Because once people respond to a version of you, that version becomes a standard.

And standards create pressure. Pressure to repeat the tone, the angle, and the feeling.

People do not want you. They want what you did for them.

This is where identity starts shrinking.

Not because the person is shallow, but because the audience is specific. The internet rewards clarity over complexity. It prefers a single note over a full range. Nuance does not travel well. Consistency does.

So people learn quickly what version of themselves works.

They start asking quieter questions: *Should I keep talking like that? Should I keep leaning into this angle? Should I stay in that lane?*

These questions do not sound dangerous. They sound strategic. Responsible even. But underneath them is a subtle trade.

Depth for repetition. Growth for familiarity. Truth for expectation.

When one moment becomes the reference point, everything else is measured against it: *Did this perform like that one did? Did this land the same way? Why did this not hit as hard?*

The person starts chasing themselves.

Not who they are now, but who they were when the internet cared the most.

This is the part no one warns about.

Going viral freezes a version of a person in public memory. And once frozen, it resists change. Growth confuses the audience. Evolution disrupts the brand. Complexity dilutes the message.

So people stay. They stay in the tone that worked, in the emotion that traveled, in the posture that brought attention.

Not because they are dishonest, but because they are rewarded for consistency rather than honesty.

Over time, the gap between the internal self and the public self widens.

Offline, the person grows. Learns. Softens. Changes. Online, the audience wants the old version–the louder version, sharper version, the version that went viral.

This creates a quiet tension.

The person feels boxed in by the very thing that elevated them. They feel pressure to perform a past self rather than expressing a present one. They begin editing themselves not based on alignment, but based on expectation.

That editing is exhausting. It is also addictive.

Because every time they lean into the viral version and the audience responds, relief returns. The body remembers the original spike. The nervous system associates that posture with safety.

So they keep going.

This is how identity becomes a loop.

The person is no longer asking who they are becoming. They are asking how to stay relevant. How to stay visible. How to keep the reaction alive.

Relevance replaces resonance. And resonance requires depth.

This is why many people who go viral feel strangely hollow afterward. On the outside, things look successful. Numbers are up. Recognition is high. But internally, something feels off.

They are being seen, but not as themselves. They are being recognized, but not for who they are now.

The internet rewards moments, not arcs. It does not follow your development; follows your highlights. And when highlights become the whole story, people lose permission to be human.

Mistakes feel riskier. Growth feels dangerous. Silence feels like falling off.

This is where anxiety enters.

The pressure to maintain relevance turns every post into a test. Every pause is a threat. Every shift is a gamble.

People stop experimenting. They stop exploring. They stop allowing themselves to be unknown.

Because the audience already decided who they are.

And deviating from that identity feels like betrayal.

This is especially destabilizing for people who already struggle with self-definition. For someone who never had a strong internal grounding, virality can feel like identity being handed to them fully formed.

Here you are. This is who you are now. That can feel comforting. Until it isn't.

Because borrowed identity does not grow with you. It demands loyalty. It demands repetition. It demands that you stay the same, so the audience does not have to adjust.

And staying the same is incompatible with being alive.

People begin performing instead of living.

They start measuring days by engagement. Moods by metrics. Worth by response. When a post under performs, it feels personal. When a post hits, it feels stabilizing.

This is not narcissism. It is conditioning.

The viral moment taught the nervous system something powerful: *This version of me is safe.*

So when life changes, when beliefs shift, when priorities evolve, the body resists. It wants the old relief. The old reaction. The old proof.

That is why people cling to who they were when they went viral. Not because that version is truer, but because that version was rewarded. This is where many creators get stuck.

They are no longer growing. They are maintaining. Protecting a moment instead of developing a life. They feel pressure to stay relevant rather than pressure to stay honest.

And over time, that pressure becomes suffocating.

People feel trapped by their own success. Afraid to disappoint an audience that does not actually know them. Afraid to change because change threatens attention.

This is the hidden cost of virality. It does not just bring attention. It brings expectation.

And expectation reshapes identity faster than most people realize.

Social media did not create this dynamic. It accelerated it. It turned moments into brands and brands into prisons.

Going viral is not dangerous because it brings attention. It is dangerous because it tempts people to confuse a moment with a self. And once that confusion sets in, growth feels like risk.

This chapter matters because it explains why people stay stuck performing versions of themselves they outgrew, why they fear silence, and why they resist change even when change is necessary.

They are not afraid of losing attention. They are afraid of losing the only version of themselves that ever felt fully seen. And until that fear is named, identity remains negotiable.

That is the real cost of going viral.

Not that it shows you to the world, but that it asks you to stay who you were when the world clapped.

5 | Turning Pain Into Performance

Pain used to be private.

Not hidden or denied, but held in smaller rooms. Shared with people who could respond with care, context, and responsibility. Healing happened slowly because it required trust. It required patience. It required boundaries.

The internet made pain became visible. And visibility changed the incentives.

Social media did not teach people to share their struggles. People have always talked about pain with one another. What changed is that pain began to perform better than peace. Vulnerability began to travel faster than stability. Exposure began to receive more reaction than resolution.

Pain became content.

At first, it feels honest.

Someone shares a hard moment, a loss, a struggle. The response is immediate: messages arrive, comments pour in, and support shows up in volume. For someone who has been carrying something heavy alone, that response feels like relief.

I am not alone. People care. I was brave enough to say it.

That relief matters.

But something subtle happens when pain gets rewarded.

The body learns that suffering produces connection. That wounds create a response. The more raw the share, the stronger the reaction.

This is where healing quietly turns into performance.

Not intentionally, not maliciously, but gradually.

Pain stops being something you process. It becomes something you present.

People begin shaping their stories around reaction. They learn which details land. Which words hit? Which emotions move the audience? They start editing their truth not for clarity, but for impact.

They do not lie. They dramatize. Because dramatization gets noticed.

This is the part no one wants to admit.

Oversharing does not always come from honesty. Sometimes it comes from regulation. From needing the reaction more than the resolution. From wanting the relief that arrives when pain is witnessed, even if it is not held.

Social media rewards expression, not integration. It amplifies disclosure, not healing.

Healing is quiet. Healing is slow. Healing does not refresh every five seconds. So it disappears.

Pain, on the other hand, performs well. It creates urgency. It invites commentary. It makes people feel involved. It gives the audience a role.

And when the audience shows up, the person sharing feels seen.

That is where the trap forms.

The body begins associating pain with connection. Struggle with relevance. Vulnerability with value.

This is not a healthy vulnerability. Healthy vulnerability is shared with people who can respond responsibly. It invites care, not consumption. It leads toward understanding, not applause.

Performance vulnerability is different.

It shares wounds without boundaries.

It is exposes before processing.

It seeks reaction, not repair.

When someone turns pain into content, they are not necessarily exploiting themselves. Often, they are trying to survive emotionally. They are trying to regulate distress using attention.

The problem is that attention does not heal wounds. It distracts from them.

Every time pain is shared publicly and rewarded, the nervous system learns a dangerous lesson.

This hurts, but it helps.

And once that lesson is learned, the incentive to heal weakens.

Because healing would remove the content.

People then begin lingering in the wound longer than necessary. They keep the story alive because the story keeps them visible. They revisit pain not to understand it, but to repackage it.

Not consciously, but habitually.

This is why some people seem stuck in their trauma. Not because they want to be, but because their trauma became their most reliable source of connection.

The internet does not ask whether someone is healing. It asks whether people are watching. And when watching becomes the metric, recovery feels risky.

What happens when I am okay? What happens when I stop sharing this? What happens when the pain resolves?

Silence threatens relevance. So pain stays public.

This dynamic creates a distortion.

The audience believes they are witnessing honesty. The creator is performing survival. Neither is malicious. But the outcome is damaging.

Pain shared without boundaries invites consumption. People comment. Speculate. Judge. Offer advice. Project their own experiences. The person sharing becomes an object of reaction instead of a subject of care.

That exposure adds pressure.

Now the person feels responsible for staying consistent with their pain. For updating the audience. For continuing the narrative. For performing the wound in a way that meets expectations.

Healing would disrupt the story. And disruption risks attention.

This is why some people feel uneasy when they start getting better. Improvement creates a loss of response. Stability gets less engagement. Peace does not travel.

So they hold onto the pain longer than they should.

This is not a weakness. It is conditioning.

The system rewards rawness without responsibility. It amplifies confession without containment. It turns wounds into entertainment and calls it authenticity.

And the audience participates.

Not intentionally, but structurally.

People are drawn to pain because pain feels real. Because pain bypasses filters. Because pain creates intimacy quickly. Watching someone suffer feels like closeness without commitment.

But closeness without commitment is not care. It is consumption. This is where the line gets crossed.

When pain becomes branding, healing becomes a threat. When trauma becomes identity, recovery feels like erasure.

People start asking *Who am I without this story?*

That question is terrifying.

Especially for those whose pain was the first thing that ever made them feel seen.

Social media did not create this dynamic. It monetized it.

It turned suffering into shareable currency and called it empowerment. It blurred the line between openness and exposure. Between telling your truth and turning your wounds into proof of relevance.

This chapter matters because it explains why people get stuck publicly bleeding instead of privately healing.

They are not addicted to pain. They are addicted to what pain gives them: attention, connection, relief.

But relief is not recovery.

Recovery requires containment. It requires privacy. It requires time away from reaction. And time away from reaction feels dangerous in an economy built on visibility.

So people keep sharing. They overshare. They rehash. They reopen wounds.

Not because they want sympathy, but because they want regulation.

The tragedy is that the very thing they use to cope prevents the thing they actually need.

Healing does not trend. But it restores. And until people understand the difference, pain will continue to be performed instead of processed.

And until people understand the difference, pain will continue to be performed instead of processed.

That is the real cost of turning wounds into content.

Not that people talk about pain, but staying inside it longer than necessary because it keeps them visible.

That is not empowerment. That is a trap.

Pain becomes currency, conflict becomes strategy, and outrage becomes even more profitable.

6 | Why Anger Always Wins

Anger travels faster than understanding.

That is not an opinion. It is a pattern. It has always been true, but social media removed the brakes. What once required proximity, escalation, and risk can now be broadcast instantly, rewarded immediately, and repeated endlessly.

Anger works because it simplifies. It reduces complexity into sides. It compresses nuance into blame. It gives people something to react to without requiring them to think.

And reaction is the currency.

In an attention economy, the emotion that creates the most movement wins. Calm does not move people. Context does not spread quickly. Patience does not provoke a response, but anger does.

Outrage activates the nervous system. It creates urgency. It makes people feel involved. It invites judgment without responsibility. You do not have to understand something to be angry about it. You only have to feel provoked.

That is why anger gets boosted.

Not because platforms prefer negativity, but because people engage with it more. They comment faster. They share more aggressively. They stay longer. They argue. They pick sides.

Engagement rises and the system responds.

What appears to be moral outrage is often chemical stimulation. The body reacts before the mind assesses. Heart rate increases. Attention narrows. The feeling feels righteous, but it is also activating.

This is why anger feels productive even when it accomplishes nothing.

It feels like action.

Social media did not invent outrage. It industrialized it.

Before, conflict had limits. It was contained by time, space, and social consequence. You argued with people you knew. You had to see them again. You had to live with what you said.

Now conflict is abstract. You fight avatars. You attack headlines. You argue with fragments of people you do not know.

The cost feels low. The reward feels high. That is the perfect environment for escalation.

Anger becomes content because it performs reliably. It does not require creativity. It does not require vulnerability. It does not require truth. It only requires reaction.

People learn quickly. If calm gets ignored and anger gets attention, the lesson is obvious.

So they lean in. At first, it feels justified. Someone did something wrong. Something needs to be called out. There is a real issue underneath the reaction.

But the response does not stay proportional.

It sharpens. Tone becomes harsher. Language becomes more extreme. Certainty replaces curiosity.

Because certainty travels better. Nuance slows people down. Anger speeds them up.

This is where fake beef starts.

Not always fake in the sense of fabricated, but exaggerated. Amplified. Prolonged beyond necessity. A conflict that could have ended privately is dragged out publicly because the engagement is too good to ignore.

People begin responding not to resolve, but to maintain momentum.

The argument becomes the content. Enemies are created because enemies drive attention. Sides are drawn because sides create loyalty. People are rewarded not for being right, but for being loud.

This creates an economy of conflict. In that economy, peace is unprofitable.

Resolution ends engagement. Understanding dissolves tension. Apologies slow things down. Growth confuses the audience.

So people stay angry. They revisit issues that could have been settled. They keep wounds open. They reframe old conflicts as ongoing wars.

Not because they enjoy anger, but because anger keeps them visible.

This is where moral performance replaces moral living.

People begin performing outrage instead of practicing values. They learn the language of justice without the work of integrity. They post statements, not solutions. They condemn publicly while doing nothing privately.

The appearance of righteousness becomes more important than the practice of it.

Because the appearance gets attention. Anger allows people to feel superior without being accountable. It offers the illusion of virtue without requiring self-examination. It externalizes blame and protects identity.

If I am angry, I must be right. If I am outraged, I must be moral. That belief is dangerous.

Because it discourages reflection. People stop asking whether their anger is proportional, informed, or useful. They only ask whether it performs.

And performance rewards escalation. This is how conversations turn into pile-ons. How disagreement turns into destruction. How people get reduced to their worst moment and frozen there.

The audience participates. They like. They comment. They share.

Not because they want harm, but because outrage feels involving. It gives them a role. It makes them feel part of something bigger than themselves.

Belonging through anger is powerful. But it is unstable because anger requires a target. Once one conflict fades, another must take its place. The feed cannot be calm. It must stay activated.

This creates exhaustion. People feel constantly on edge. Always ready to react. Always waiting for the next thing to be mad about. The nervous system never settles.

And yet, stepping back feels risky. Silence gets interpreted as complicity. Calm gets mistaken for indifference. Nuance gets labeled as a weakness.

So people stay loud. They perform anger even when they are tired of it.

This is especially dangerous for people whose identity is already tied to attention. For them, anger becomes a reliable tool. A way to stay relevant. A way to stay seen.

They are no longer responding to issues. They are maintaining a posture.

Over time, that posture hardens. Anger stops being a reaction and becomes an identity. The person is known for being outspoken, aggressive, and fearless. Those labels feel flattering. They also create a trap.

Because stepping out of character risks losing attention.

So they keep going.

Even when it no longer aligns. Even when it costs relationships. Even when it drains them.

This is the part people rarely admit.

Anger pays. It pays in engagement. It pays in visibility. It pays in relevance. But it charges interest. It costs peace. It costs nuance. It costs empathy. And eventually, it costs credibility.

Because constant outrage flattens meaning. When everything is an emergency, nothing is. When every issue is treated as a war, people stop trusting the signal.

The audience grows numb. Then the person has to escalate again: louder, sharper, and more extreme.

This is how cycles form. Not because people are cruel. Because systems reward stimulation.

Social media did not make people angry. It made anger efficient.

It removed the cost and multiplied the return.

Understanding this matters because, without it, people believe they are choosing anger freely. In reality, many are responding to incentives they barely recognize.

Anger always wins in the short term. But it loses something essential in the long term.

It replaces understanding with performance. It replaces dialogue with dominance. It replaces growth with repetition.

This chapter matters because it explains why conflict has become constant and resolution feels rare.

People are not angrier than before. They are more rewarded for staying that way. And once anger becomes currency, the character starts getting traded away.

That is where the corruption deepens.

When anger stops being enough, people begin lying to keep the attention alive.

7 | Clout Over Character

Character used to be revealed over time.

You learned who someone was by how they moved when no one was watching, by how they handled pressure, disappointment, boredom, and temptation.

Character showed up in patterns, not moments, and it required both proximity and patience.

Clout changed that.

It compresses time and shortcuts credibility, allowing people to be believed before they are known, trusted before they are tested, and rewarded before they are consistent.

That shift matters.

Because when attention arrives before character is built, people learn a dangerous lesson: *Visibility can replace integrity.*

At first, the compromise feels small.

A story gets exaggerated. A detail gets stretched. A moment gets framed a little more dramatically than it happened.

Not because the person wants to deceive, but because the truth did not hit hard enough. The reaction was muted. The numbers were underwhelming. And somewhere in the background, the nervous system remembers what a bigger reaction feels like.

So the next version gets sharper. The story becomes cleaner. The villain becomes clearer. The hero becomes more defined.

Reality is messy. Content prefers clarity.

People do not usually lie outright at the beginning. They edit. They embellish. They remove context that complicates the narrative. They add intention where there was confusion. They turn coincidence into strategy. They turn luck into grind.

It feels harmless. Everyone does it. It's just the internet. It's not that deep.

But repetition changes things.

When embellishment gets rewarded, it becomes a habit. When exaggeration performs better than accuracy, accuracy starts feeling optional. Over time, people stop asking whether something is true and start asking whether it works.

That is the pivot.

Truth becomes negotiable. Character becomes flexible. Consistency becomes less important than reaction.

This is where clout overtakes character.

Clout is fast. Character is slow. Clout rewards moments. Character requires patterns.

And in a system built on speed, slowness feels like failure.

People begin saying things they have not lived. Claiming values they have not practiced. Speaking with certainty, they have not earned. They adopt language before they adopt discipline. Identity becomes aspirational instead of grounded.

Not because they are fraudulent, but because they are incentivized to perform confidently before developing competence.

The internet does not wait for growth. It rewards projection.

So people project.

They speak like authorities on lives they have not fully navigated. They give advice that they have not integrated. They sell wisdom they have not tested under pressure.

And when challenged, they double down. Because backing up threatens the image. And the image now carries value.

This is how people get trapped defending versions of themselves they barely recognize.

The audience plays a role.

People want certainty. They want leaders. They want clean narratives. They reward people who sound sure, even when certainty is premature. They punish hesitation. They mistake humility for weakness.

So the loudest voices rise. And the quiet, consistent ones disappear.

Over time, people learn that character does not trend. Integrity does not spike metrics. Restraint does not go viral. Saying "I don't know" does not perform.

So people stop saying it. They stop leaving room for doubt. They stop acknowledging complexity. They stop admitting growth.

Because growth implies past ignorance. And past ignorance threatens authority.

This creates a strange inversion.

People who are still becoming present themselves as complete. People who are unsure speak with absolute conviction. People who are inconsistent brand themselves as unwavering.

The performance becomes heavier than the person carrying it.

Internally, this creates tension. The person knows who they really are. They know what they have skipped. They know what they exaggerated.

But externally, they are rewarded for the image they project.

So they protect it. They curate their life around it. They avoid situations that might expose gaps. They deflect questions that challenge the narrative. They surround themselves with people who reinforce the version they are selling.

Not intentionally at first, but gradually.

This is how clout isolates.

The higher someone climbs on an image that is not fully grounded, the more fragile they become. Every contradiction feels dangerous. Every mistake feels catastrophic. Every challenge feels personal.

This is where fear enters: fear of being exposed, fear of being called out, fear of being seen clearly. And fear drives behavior.

People preemptively attack critics, discredit anyone who questions them, and frame accountability as hate because if character collapses, clout disappears with it.

This is why some people become defensive instead of reflective. Why they will explain instead of examine. Why they will perform morality instead of practicing it.

The goal shifts from being good to being seen as good.

And being seen as good is easier. You can post the right phrases, adopt the right stances, align with the right moments. You do not have to live them.

Living values is quiet. Posting values is loud. Loud wins.

But character has a way of resurfacing.

Eventually, the gaps show. Stories stop lining up, behavior contradicts branding, and pressure exposes what was never built.

And when that happens, the fall is harder than the rise because the audience was not connected to the person. They were connected to the image.

Images collapse quickly.

This is where people say they were misunderstood. That the internet is fake. That people turned on them.

Sometimes that is true. Sometimes the internet did not change. The mask slipped.

This chapter matters because it explains why so many public figures seem hollow behind the scenes. Why confidence feels so brittle. Why success feels fragile.

It is not because they are bad people. It is because clout asked them to skip steps. And steps skipped in character development do not disappear. They wait.

They wait until pressure arrives. They wait until temptation shows up. They wait until the audience demands consistency. Then they surface.

Social media did not create dishonesty. It rewarded performance faster than integrity could be built.

And when performance becomes the primary currency, character becomes negotiable.

That is the corruption. Not that people lie, but that truth becomes optional when attention is on the line.

And once truth is optional, identity becomes unstable.

This is why people eventually feel like they are living someone else's life. Defending someone else's values. Protecting an image they no longer recognize.

Clout feels powerful at first, but it is light. Character is heavy. It takes time, it takes friction, it takes humility.

And anything that bypasses that weight eventually collapses under it.

That is the cost of choosing clout over character. Not public failure, but internal erosion.

And erosion is harder to see until there is nothing left to stand on.

8 | Love as Leverage

Love used to be lived.

It happened in private spaces. In shared routines. In arguments that stayed between the people, having them. Relationships grew quietly because they required trust, repair, and patience. Even when they failed, they failed out of sight.

Then relationships became visible.

And visibility changed the terms.

Social media did not invent sharing your life. People have always talked about love. What changed was that love began to attract attention. Intimacy began producing engagement. And once engagement entered the relationship, the relationship stopped belonging only to the people inside it.

Love became content.

At first, it feels harmless.

A couple posts a photo. People respond. Compliments arrive. The relationship feels affirmed. Supported. Celebrated. For people who never felt chosen publicly, that affirmation feels powerful.

We look good together. People see us. This Matters.

That response reinforces something subtle: *Being loved publicly feels safer than being loved privately.*

And once that belief forms, the audience becomes part of the relationship.

That is where the problem starts.

Because audiences do not want nuance. They want storylines. They want progression. They want drama. They want highs and lows they can react to.

Good relationships are not built for spectators, but conflict means clicks.

So when tension appears, people share it. Not to resolve it, but to be seen inside it. They post cryptic captions. Emotional videos. Half stories. Enough detail to provoke reaction, not enough to create understanding.

The audience fills in the gaps. They take sides, offer opinions, and validate pain without context.

The person posting feels supported, but that support comes at a cost.

Because now the relationship is no longer just between two people. It is between two people and thousands of interpretations.

Private conflict becomes public leverage.

People begin using attention as reinforcement. When they feel unseen in the relationship, they turn to the audience. When they feel hurt, they broadcast. When they feel lonely, they post.

Not to heal. To regulate.

The internet becomes a third party in the relationship.

And third parties are not responsible for outcomes.

They leave when the story gets boring. They move on when the narrative shifts. They do not stay to help repair what they have inflamed.

This dynamic quietly erodes trust.

Partners begin feeling exposed. Conversations that should have stayed private become public record. Vulnerability becomes risky. Mistakes feel dangerous.

People stop speaking honestly. They start performing pain instead of expressing it. This is how intimacy dies publicly while appearing alive online.

Breakups become content.

Not always planned. Often reactive.

Someone posts through heartbreak. The response is overwhelming. Support pours in. Validation arrives quickly. The person feels held by strangers while the actual relationship dissolves quietly behind the scenes.

The audience sees a hero and a villain; reality is rarely that clean. But complexity does not trend.

So one person becomes the bad guy. One becomes the survivor. The narrative hardens. The relationship becomes frozen in a version that feels final even if the truth is unfinished.

This makes reconciliation almost impossible, as healing privately would contradict the public story. Contradicting the story risks attention, so people commit to the narrative instead of the truth.

This is especially damaging when children are involved.

Children become content before they become conscious. Their lives get documented, shared, and commented on. Their pain becomes engagement. Their milestones become metrics.

Parents justify it as sharing joy, but attention changes the energy. Moments become staged, reactions become expected, and privacy disappears before consent exists.

Children learn early that love comes with cameras. That affection is performative. Those family moments are for public consumption.

They do not get to choose that lesson. And once it is taught, it is hard to undo.

This is not about posting photos of your life.

It is about using relationships as leverage.

When love becomes proof of worth, when heartbreak becomes validation, when intimacy becomes a tool for relevance. The relationship stops being a place of refuge. It becomes a stage. And stages demand performance.

People stay in relationships longer than they should because leaving would disrupt the image. Others leave faster than they should because the breakup performs better than the repair.

Decisions are shaped by reaction instead of reflection.

The question shifts from *What is healthy for us?* to *What will people think?*

That shift is quiet. But it is corrosive.

Partners begin to feel like characters instead of humans. Like symbols instead of individuals. Like supporting roles in someone else's storyline.

Love cannot survive that pressure. Because love requires safety. And safety disappears when everything is public.

This is why so many relationships look strong online and feel empty offline. Why couples seem perfect until they suddenly collapse. Why breakups feel shocking to audiences but inevitable to the people inside them.

The relationship was never nurtured. It was maintained. Maintained for perception, maintained for relevance, maintained for applause.

Social media did not destroy relationships.

It rewarded exposure over protection.

It encouraged people to trade privacy for validation. To use love as proof of value instead of practicing it as a commitment. Wen love becomes leverage, authenticity disappears.

People stop asking *How do we grow?* and start asking *How do we look?*

That question kills intimacy slowly. Because intimacy is not impressive. It is not flashy. It does not trend. Intimacy happens when no one is watching.

And that is exactly what the attention economy discourages.

This chapter matters because it explains why so many people feel lonely in relationships that look full online. Why public affection does not translate into private security. Why being loved loudly does not feel the same as being loved well.

Attention can amplify love, but it cannot replace care.

When people confuse the two, relationships become transactions instead of bonds. Moments become content instead of connection. And love becomes something to use instead of something to protect.

That is the corruption.

Once relationships are used for attention, they stop being safe. And when safety disappears, people either perform harder or leave louder. Both of which are symptoms of the same mistake.

Treating love like leverage in a system that does not care what breaks.

And once love breaks publicly, people learn a dangerous lesson: *Privacy is weakness. Silence is failure. Healing is boring.*

Those lessons do not stay inside relationships.

They spill into everything else.

Which is why fear becomes the next currency.

9 | The Fear Economy

Fear keeps people quiet.

Not always silent, but careful. Measured. Strategic. Fear does not scream. It watches. It waits. It calculates. And in the attention economy, fear has become one of the most powerful currencies in circulation.

Cancel culture did not begin as punishment. It began as accountability. A collective attempt to call out harm, correct behavior, and protect people from abuse. At its core, it was rooted in responsibility.

But accountability requires proportion. And proportion does not perform. Fear does.

Over time, the line between correction and destruction blurred. Mistakes stopped being moments and started becoming identities. Context disappeared and growth became irrelevant. People were frozen in their worst actions and displayed as warnings.

This is how the fear economy formed.

Everyone is watching. Everyone is waiting. Everyone is recording. Not to understand. To catch.

In this environment, people do not ask what is right. They ask what is safe. They do not speak from clarity. They speak with calculation.

Can I say this? Should I say this? Will this be misunderstood? Will this cost me?

Fear reshapes behavior quietly.

People begin performing morality instead of living it. They learn the language of righteousness without doing the internal work of integrity. They post the right statements at the right times. They echo approved opinions. They align publicly even when privately unsure.

Not because they are dishonest. Because they are afraid.

The fear is not irrational. The consequences are real.

One sentence taken out of context can erase years of consistency. One old post can resurface and completely redefine someone. One misstep can trigger a wave that feels impossible to outrun.

And because the internet has no expiration date, mistakes do not fade. They wait.

This creates hyper vigilance.

People edit themselves constantly. They sanitize opinions. They flatten complexity. They remove nuance before it can be misunderstood. They stop exploring ideas out loud.

Curiosity becomes risky. Questioning becomes dangerous. Silence becomes safer.

But silence has a cost.

When people stop speaking honestly, they stop thinking honestly. When expression is filtered through fear, growth stalls. People begin confusing safety with alignment. Agreement with integrity.

They choose caution over clarity, and while caution can protect in the short term, it erodes authenticity over time.

This is how fear becomes structural.

Not enforced by any single authority, but by anticipation: the anticipation of backlash, of judgment, of being misunderstood publicly and permanently.

Fear does not require actual cancellation to function. It only requires the possibility.

That possibility shapes behavior. People watch others fall and take notes, observing what language gets punished, what opinions get dragged, what silence gets questioned. They adjust accordingly.

The result is a culture where people are not being themselves. They are being acceptable.

Acceptability becomes the goal. Not truth, not growth, not honesty. Acceptability.

This creates a strange contradiction.

Everyone is talking, but fewer people say anything real.

Feeds are loud, but conversation is shallow. Opinions sound identical. Language becomes scripted. Everyone knows the right words to say, but few are willing to explore what they actually believe.

Fear creates conformity. And conformity feels like safety.

But safety built on suppression does not last. Internally, people feel the tension.

They feel dishonest for not speaking fully, anxious about not knowing what is allowed, and exhausted from constant self-monitoring.

This is why so many people feel drained online, even when they are not posting much.

Fear is heavy. Carrying it requires energy.

Fear also distorts morality.

When people are more afraid of being wrong publicly than being wrong privately, ethics become performative. Apologies become strategic. Accountability becomes transactional.

People stop asking how to grow and start asking how to survive.

This is how moral performance replaces moral living.

People say the right things without integrating them. They align with causes without practicing the values they espouse. They condemn others publicly while avoiding their self-reflection.

Not because they are hypocrites, but because fear discourages introspection.

Looking inward is dangerous when the audience is waiting to pounce.

So people look outward instead. They police others, call out strangers, and amplify outrage.

Because attacking feels safer than being exposed.

Fear creates aggressors and silencers.

Some people go quiet, some go loud. Both are responding to the same pressure.

The system rewards those who enforce the rules. It punishes those who violate them. And the rules are often unclear, shifting, and inconsistently applied.

That uncertainty keeps people on edge.

In this environment, growth feels risky.

If changing your mind can be framed as inconsistency, if learning can be framed as ignorance, if evolving can be framed as betrayal, then staying the same feels safer.

So people freeze. They cling to positions they've outgrown, defend statements they no longer believe, and double down instead of backing up.

Fear locks identity in place, and locked identities do not grow.

This is why so many people feel trapped inside versions of themselves they no longer align with. Why discourse feels brittle. Why mistakes feel fatal.

People are not afraid of accountability. They are afraid of erasure: erasure from community, from relevance, from belonging.

Because belonging has been made conditional.

Say the right things, think the right thoughts, move at the right pace. Or risk exile.

This is not justice. It's fear management.

And fear management does not create better people. It creates quieter ones. More anxious ones. More performative ones.

Social media did not create fear. It scaled it.

It turned accountability into spectacle. It made punishment public and growth invisible. It rewarded outrage and ignored repair.

Fear keeps engagement high. Calm does not.

This is why fear persists.

This chapter is not an argument against accountability. Accountability matters. Harm should be addressed. Responsibility should be taken.

But accountability without room for growth becomes control, and control does not heal culture. It fractures it.

When people are afraid to be human, they stop being honest. When honesty disappears, trust follows.

That is the real damage of the fear economy.

And once fear replaces curiosity, attention replaces truth, and survival replaces integrity, the system sustains itself.

That is where the cycle deepens.

Because when people are afraid to be wrong, they cling harder to validation, and validation becomes identity.

10 | When Validation Becomes Identity

At some point, attention stops being something you receive. It becomes something you rely on.

This is the moment people rarely notice while it's happening. There's no announcement, no dramatic shift. Just a quiet change in how the self is held. The internal sense of who you are begins leaning outward. You start checking the room before checking yourself, measuring worth by response instead of alignment.

And once that happens, validation is no longer feedback. It is identity.

The question is no longer *Did this land?* It becomes *Do I exist if it doesn't?*

This is where things get dangerous.

Because identity is meant to be stable. It's supposed to hold under pressure. It's built through consistency, values, discipline, and lived experience. Validation, on the other hand, is volatile. It fluctuates. It depends on mood, timing, audience, and algorithm.

When identity is built on something unstable, the self becomes unstable.

People begin waking up thinking about reaction. They plan their day around posting windows. They feel uneasy when they're offline for too long. Not bored. Not lonely. Unreal.

If nothing is being shared, nothing feels confirmed.

This is where silence starts to feel threatening. Not peaceful. Not grounding. Threatening.

Silence becomes absence, absence becomes erasure, and erasure feels like losing yourself.

People do not say this out loud. They say things like *I just like being connected. I enjoy sharing. This is how I express myself.*

Those things can be true. But when expression becomes necessary for self-confirmation, something has shifted.

Posting stops being creative. It becomes compulsive.

The person is no longer asking what they want to say. They're asking what will land. They're no longer checking whether something feels true. They're checking whether it will be received.

Identity moves from internal to external, and once that happens, the self becomes responsive instead of grounded.

People begin adjusting their personality based on feedback. They soften when softness gets praised. They harden when sharpness gets rewarded. They exaggerate traits that perform and suppress those that do not.

Not intentionally. Automatically.

This is how people lose themselves without realizing they ever left.

Because nothing disappears all at once. It erodes.

A little less honesty here. A little more performance there. A little less silence. A little more noise.

Over time, the original self becomes quieter, and when it is quiet long enough, people start feeling empty even when they're visible.

This is the paradox. They're being seen by thousands, but they don't feel known by themselves.

The identity has been outsourced. The internet becomes the mirror.

And mirrors that constantly refresh do not reflect depth. They reflect reaction.

This is why people feel anxious when engagement drops. It's not about ego. It's about destabilization. The mirror is not responding the way it usually does. The reflection feels distorted.

People start asking questions that sound shallow but are deeply psychological: *Did I fall off? Am I still relevant? Do people still care?*

But they're really asking *Am I still here?*

Because when validation becomes identity, metrics become proof of existence.

This is where silence starts to feel like death. Not literal death. Identity death.

The version of self that lives online requires maintenance. It must be fed regularly. If it's not, it begins to disappear, and disappearance feels like loss.

And disappearance feels like loss.

So people post when they're tired. Post when they're empty. Post when they have nothing to say. Not to express. To confirm.

This is where burnout gets misunderstood. People think burnout comes from posting too much. Burnout comes from needing to post.

It comes from having no internal place to return to when the reaction stops.

People say they need a break from social media. But what they really need is a break from the identity they built there.

Because that identity demands constant proof. It demands performance, relevance, and consistency without rest.

And identities that demand proof are always fragile.

This is why criticism hits harder when validation becomes identity. It's not just feedback. It feels like a threat to the self. A disagreement feels like rejection. A correction feels like an attack.

People respond defensively. Not because they're arrogant. Because they're exposed.

When the self is externalized, any negative reaction feels personal. There's no internal buffer. No grounded place to stand.

So people protect the image aggressively. They explain instead of reflect, justify instead of listen, and block instead of consider.

Not because they're unwilling to grow. Because growth threatens the version of themselves that receives validation.

This is how people get stuck. They can't change without risking relevance. They can't be silent without feeling erased. They can't evolve without destabilizing their identity.

So they stay. They repeat. They perform. They maintain.

And maintenance replaces meaning.

The self becomes something to manage instead of something to live from.

This is why so many people say they feel disconnected from themselves. Why they struggle to answer simple questions offline. Why they feel restless without their phone. Why they feel undefined without an audience.

They're not addicted to social media. They're dependent on external confirmation to know who they are.

This chapter matters because it explains why leaving feels impossible.

When validation becomes identity, logging off feels like disappearing. Slowing down feels like fading out. Silence feels like losing ground.

People aren't afraid of missing out. They're afraid of no longer existing in the way they learned to exist.

This is the psychological prison.

Because once the self is built externally, there's no internal home to return to.

Everything depends on the reaction, and reactions are unpredictable.

Which means the self is never settled. Never finished. Never safe. Always waiting.

Waiting for the next notification. The next response. The next proof.

That's not identity. That's dependency.

And dependency reshapes everything that follows.

It changes how people post, how they speak, how they love, how they think.

And most importantly, how they sit with themselves when no one is watching.

Because when validation becomes identity, being alone is no longer restful. It's terrifying.

That fear is what keeps people posting long after the joy has gone.

And until that fear is understood, no advice will free anyone from it.

Because you cannot walk away from something you believe is keeping you alive.

That is the trap.

And now that the trap is clear, the next chapters will show why the system itself makes it so hard to escape.

Not because it hates you. But because it doesn't care who you become.

11 | Algorithms Do Not Care About You

Algorithms don't have values. They don't have morals. They don't have memory. They don't have concern for your well-being. They are not cruel. They are not malicious. They are indifferent.

This is important because many people personalize what is happening to them online. They feel rejected when engagement drops. They feel rewarded when numbers rise. They interpret performance as affirmation and silence as judgment.

But algorithms aren't responding to you. They're responding to behavior.

Specifically, they respond to what keeps people engaged.

The system is simple. What holds attention gets shown more. What doesn't disappears. That's it. No nuance. No loyalty. No concern for balance.

Calm doesn't hold people. Extremes do.

Nuance requires time. Outrage demands reaction. So outrage spreads.

This isn't because platforms prefer chaos. It's because chaos keeps people scrolling. It activates the nervous system. It shortens attention spans while increasing time spent.

The algorithm doesn't ask whether something is healthy. It asks whether it keeps eyes on the screen.

That question shapes everything.

Creators feel this pressure even when they cannot articulate it. They notice which posts land. Which tones get boosted. Which emotions spike metrics. Over time, they adjust.

Not because they want to be extreme. Because the system rewards it.

Balanced takes get buried. Thoughtful reflection gets ignored. Measured language fades.

So people sharpen. They simplify. They polarize.

Not because they believe more deeply, but because they want to remain visible.

This is where people misunderstand the trap. They think they're choosing intensity. In reality, intensity is being selected for them.

The algorithm trains behavior through feedback. It amplifies what performs and starves what does not. Over time, creators internalize the rules even when they resent them.

They know what works. And knowing what works changes what you're willing to say.

People stop exploring ideas that require patience. They avoid topics that invite complexity. They choose certainty over curiosity because certainty travels faster.

This isn't about truth. It's about traction.

The algorithm doesn't reward honesty. It rewards engagement. Sometimes those overlap. Often they don't.

This is why people feel pressured to exaggerate their emotions. To react louder than they feel. To speak in absolutes instead of questions.

They're not trying to deceive. They're trying to survive the feed.

The danger isn't that algorithms exist. The danger is that people begin modeling their identity around something that has no stake in their humanity.

Algorithms don't care if you burn out. They don't care if you lose relationships. They don't care if you distort yourself to stay visible.

They will keep rewarding what keeps attention moving.

And when something stops working, they move on.

Creators often describe this as a 'fall off'. But falling off isn't personal. It's structural.

It is structural.

The algorithm didn't reject you. It found something more stimulating.

That realization is destabilizing.

Because when your identity is tied to validation, and validation is controlled by something indifferent, the self becomes unstable.

People chase the algorithm. They try new tones. New angles. New extremes.

They refresh constantly. Not because they're greedy. Because silence feels dangerous.

This is where balance becomes invisible. Healthy expression doesn't spike engagement. Moderation doesn't trend. Growth doesn't come with applause.

So people feel punished for calming down. They feel ignored when they heal. They feel invisible when they stabilize.

That invisibility feels like a loss.

This is why people relapse into old patterns. Why they return to outrage. Why they revisit pain. Why they resurrect conflict.

Because those things still work.

The algorithm doesn't know that you're tired. It doesn't know that you have outgrown a version of yourself. It only knows that version once kept people watching.

So it keeps asking for it.

This creates a cruel loop. The person wants peace. The system rewards stimulation. The person wants growth. The system rewards repetition. The person wants depth. The system rewards simplicity.

And because attention has already become identity, resisting the algorithm feels like self-sabotage.

People say they want to slow down, but they are afraid of disappearing.

That fear is not irrational. Because the system is built to move on.

It does not wait. It does not check in. It does not care.

Understanding this matters because it removes the illusion of control.

You're not in a relationship with the algorithm. You're in a transaction.

And transactions do not love you back.

Once people understand that, they can stop taking performance personally. They can stop equating engagement with worth. They can stop chasing a system that cannot reciprocate.

But until that understanding is solid, people keep adjusting themselves to please something that has no loyalty.

That's the trap. Algorithms are not villains. But they are not caretakers.

And building your identity inside something that does not care about you guarantees instability.

This chapter matters because it explains why balance feels punished, and extremity feels rewarded. Why people feel pressure to stay sharp even when they want to soften.

The system is not asking who you are. It's asking what keeps people watching.

And if you confuse those two questions, you will eventually lose yourself trying to answer the wrong one.

That loss is not dramatic. It's quiet.

It happens when you stop trusting your internal compass and start following feedback that refreshes every second.

Algorithms do not care about you. They care about attention.

And attention does not care what it costs you.

That is why leaving feels so hard.

And why the pressure to stay relevant becomes the next weight people carry.

12 | The Pressure to Stay Relevant

Relevance is not a goal anyone sets out with honestly.

People do not wake up thinking, I want to be relevant. They wake up wanting to matter. To be seen. To not disappear. Relevance sneaks in later, disguised as consistency, discipline, or ambition.

By the time people realize they are chasing relevance, they are already afraid of losing it.

Staying relevant doesn't feel like winning. It feels like maintaining. And maintenance is exhausting.

Once someone experiences attention consistently, the absence of it starts feeling like failure. Not because anything bad has happened, but because something expected did not. The feed moved on. The response softened. The numbers dipped.

The body notices. Fear enters quietly.

Did I fall off? Did people lose interest? Am I still in the conversation?

These questions are rarely asked out loud. They live in the background, shaping behavior subtly. People don't post because they have something to say. They post because they feel pressure to stay present.

Presence becomes proof: *if I am visible, I still exist. If I disappear, I am forgotten.*

This is where posting becomes compulsory.

People share when they're tired. They create when they're empty. They perform when they have nothing left to give. Not because they want to. Because slowing down feels dangerous.

Relevance doesn't allow rest. The moment you pause, someone else fills the space. The feed doesn't wait. The algorithm does not hold your place. Silence does not signal depth. It signals absence.

So people push. They stretch stories. They force opinions. They manufacture urgency. Anything to stay in motion.

This pressure distorts intention.

Instead of asking what feels true, people ask what feels timely. Instead of expressing what matters, they chase what is trending. They stop listening inward and start scanning outward.

What are people reacting to? What is blowing up? What can I comment on?

Relevance rewards responsiveness, not reflection. That's the trade.

People become commentators on everything instead of participants in their own lives. They react to headlines they haven't processed. They form opinions before understanding. They speak constantly to avoid silence.

Because silence feels like falling behind.

This is where meaning gets lost.

When relevance becomes the priority, depth becomes a liability. Thoughtfulness slows output. Complexity dilutes reaction. Growth disrupts consistency.

So people stay surface level. They repeat familiar takes. They recycle old emotions. They revisit past conflicts. Not because they're stuck. Because the system rewards predictability.

The fear of falling off reshapes identity.

People stop evolving publicly. They freeze their personality at whatever version brought attention. They fear experimenting because experiments can fail.

Failure feels public. Failure feels permanent. So they play it safe.

Ironically, staying relevant often requires becoming less real.

People begin measuring their days by engagement, their moods by metrics, their worth by response. . When a post underperforms, it feels personal. When it performs, it feels stabilizing.

But that stability is temporary. Relevance is fragile. It demands constant proof. It must be fed regularly. And it never assures you it'll stay.

This creates a background anxiety that never fully leaves.

Even when things are going well, people are waiting for the drop, waiting for the moment the audience moves on, waiting for the algorithm to change.

This anticipation is exhausting.

It drains creativity. It flattens emotion. It replaces joy with vigilance.

People say they love what they do, but they're tired all the time. They say they're grateful, but they feel restless. They say they're fulfilled, but they feel hollow.

Because relevance doesn't nourish. It depletes.

The pressure to stay relevant also distorts self-worth.

People stop asking whether their work is meaningful. They ask whether it is visible. They stop evaluating their growth internally and start measuring it externally.

The question shifts from *Am I becoming better?* to *Am I still being seen?*

This subtle shift changes everything.

It makes people dependent on external cues to feel grounded, makes silence intolerable, and makes rest feel irresponsible.

Rest becomes risky. *What if you miss the moment? What if you lose momentum? What if you're replaced?*

This fear keeps people moving long after they should stop.

And because relevance is public, the pressure feels communal. People watch peers rise and fall, compare trajectories, track numbers, and internalize other people's visibility as commentary on their own.

Comparison intensifies.

This chapter matters because it explains why people can't slow down even when they want to. Why they keep posting even when the joy is gone. Why relevance feels like oxygen instead of exposure.

People are not afraid of obscurity. They're afraid of becoming invisible again. Especially if invisibility once hurt.

Relevance promises protection from that pain.

But protection built on attention is fragile.

Because relevance doesn't care who you are. It only cares whether you're still being noticed.

And when being noticed becomes the goal, meaning becomes secondary.

That's the cost of staying relevant. Not failure. Erosion. Erosion of intention. Erosion of depth. Erosion of self.

And erosion is hardest to notice while it's happening. Because you're too busy keeping up.

Because once relevance becomes the chase, comparison becomes the poison that keeps it alive.

13 | Comparison Is the Quiet Killer

Comparison does not announce itself.

It slips in quietly, disguised as inspiration. Someone else's success shows up on your screen, and for a moment, it feels motivating. You admire it. You respect it. You tell yourself you're happy for them.

Then something shifts. The comparison begins.

Why them? Why not me? Why faster? Why louder?

Comparison rarely arrives as jealousy. It arrives as a measurement. As an evaluation. As a silent audit of where you stand.

And because social media collapses distance, comparison is constant.

You are no longer comparing yourself to a few peers. You're comparing yourself to thousands of curated lives, edited highlights, and perfectly timed wins. You're comparing your full reality to everyone else's best moment.

That imbalance is devastating.

Offline, comparison had limits. You saw people you knew. You understood the context. You saw their flaws, their struggles, their setbacks. Online, context disappears. All you see is momentum.

Wins stacked on wins. Smiles without exhaustion. Success without the cost.

And the brain fills in the gaps. Everyone else is winning. Everyone else figured it out. *I am behind.*

That thought settles quietly, but it lingers.

Comparison creates dissatisfaction even when nothing's wrong.

People can be doing well and still feel inadequate. They can be growing and still feel stuck. They can be accomplished and still feel small.

Because comparison reframes progress as failure.

When someone else's highlight outshines your day, your day starts feeling insufficient.

When someone else's growth looks faster, your pace feels embarrassing.

This is not because you're failing. It's because you're watching too much.

Comparison steals joy by shifting attention outward. It makes people lose sight of their own trajectory. It turns growth into competition.

And competition is exhausting when the rules are unclear.

Social media doesn't show the full race. It shows moments. Bursts. Peaks. You're comparing your entire process to someone else's outcome.

That will always feel unfair. Comparison also distorts perception of self-worth.

People begin tying their value to relative position. Not who they are, but where they rank. Not what they are building, but how it looks compared to others.

This creates quiet resentment.

Not always toward others.

Toward self.

Why am I not further? Why am I not bigger? Why am I not more?

These questions sound like ambition, but they are fueled by comparison.

And comparison never leads to satisfaction. There's always someone ahead. Always someone louder. Always someone trending.

So the measuring never ends. This is why people feel depressed in rooms full of success. Why abundance doesn't feel like enough. Why achievement still feels hollow.

Because comparison erases gratitude. It makes progress invisible. It turns milestones into reminders of what you haven't reached yet.

This is especially dangerous when relevance is already the goal.

People begin chasing other people's timelines instead of honoring their own. They rush growth. They skip steps. They take shortcuts. They force outcomes before they are ready.

Not because they're impatient. Because comparison creates urgency.

It whispers that time is running out. That if you don't move faster, you'll be left behind. That if you're not visible now, you never will be.

This urgency pushes people into misalignment.

They pursue things they don't actually want. They adopt aesthetics that don't fit. They speak in voices that aren't theirs. They mold themselves to trends instead of truth.

Not consciously. Desperately.

Comparison also poisons relationships.

People stop celebrating others fully because celebration triggers self-judgment. They offer support while secretly feeling diminished. They distance themselves from people who are doing well because proximity amplifies comparison.

This creates isolation.

Success becomes lonely. Struggle becomes private.

Everyone is performing strength while quietly measuring themselves against each other.

This is the quiet violence of comparison. It doesn't shout. It whispers.

It tells you that you're late. That you're behind. That your pace is wrong.

And because the feed never stops, the whisper never quiets.

Even rest becomes comparative. People compare vacations. Bodies. Relationships. Healing journeys.

Nothing is allowed to exist without being ranked. This constant ranking erodes self-trust.

People stop listening to their internal compass. They start adjusting based on external benchmarks. They make decisions not because something feels right, but because someone else already did it.

Comparison replaces intuition. And intuition is fragile.

Once it's drowned out long enough, people forget how to hear it. This is why success online often feels like failure internally.

You hit milestones but feel unsatisfied. You grow but feel anxious. You achieve but feel behind.

Because comparison keeps moving the finish line.

There's no arrival point. Just new reference points.

Social media didn't create comparison. It made it unavoidable.

It turned private measurement into a public spectacle. It allowed everyone to see everyone else's progress in real time, without context, without nuance, without pause.

The result is chronic dissatisfaction.

People aren't unhappy because they're doing poorly. They're unhappy because they're measuring themselves against illusions.

This chapter matters because comparison is one of the most powerful drivers of self-erasure.

It kills joy quietly. It undermines confidence subtly. It drains motivation slowly.

And by the time people realize it's happening, they've already adjusted their identity around it.

They are no longer asking *What do I want?* They are asking *How do I stack up?*

That question never has a satisfying answer.

Because someone will always be ahead. And until people stop confusing visibility with progress, comparison will continue to poison self-esteem.

This is why the next chapter matters.

Because when comparison runs long enough, it doesn't just distort perception. It creates a crash.

A moment when attention fades, comparison quiets, and people are left alone with a self they have not been listening to.

That moment is where the applause stops.

And the cost finally shows up.

14 | The Crash After the Applause

The crash does not come when attention disappears.

It comes when attention fades.

That difference matters.

Disappearance is sudden. It shocks. It announces itself. Fading is quieter. Slower. It gives just enough reaction to keep hope alive while taking enough away to create anxiety.

The applause doesn't stop all at once. It thins. A little less engagement. A little less excitement. A little less urgency around your presence.

Nothing dramatic enough to justify panic, nothing stable enough to feel secure.

This is where the crash begins.

For people whose identity has been built around validation, the fading feels personal. It doesn't register as a shift in audience behavior or algorithmic cycles. It registers as loss.

Something is wrong with me. I am slipping. I am being replaced.

That internal narrative is devastating.

Because the attention once felt like proof of worth. And when proof weakens, worth feels threatened.

The body reacts before the mind can reason: anxiety rises, sleep gets lighter, the urge to post increases.

People refresh obsessively. They check metrics they used to glance at. They look for explanations. They scan their content for mistakes.

What did I do wrong? What changed? How do I fix this?

The crash is not just emotional. It is physiological.

The nervous system has been conditioned to receive regulation from reaction. When the reaction drops, the body experiences withdrawal—not metaphorically.

Literally.

Restlessness sets in. Irritability. Emptiness. A low-level panic that has no clear source.

People often mislabel this moment. They call it burnout. They call it depression. They call it boredom.

But what they are feeling is the absence of an external regulator they depended on.

Attention had become medicine. Now the dosage has been reduced.

This is why the crash feels disproportionate to what is actually happening. From the outside, everything looks fine. The person still has followers. Still has reach. Still has visibility.

But internally, the body remembers the peak. And anything less feels like a loss.

This is where people make desperate choices.

They return to old versions of themselves. They revisit conflict. They reopen wounds.

Not because those things feel good. Because they still work.

People resurrect past pain because it once brought a response. They reenter arguments they had resolved. They exaggerate emotions they no longer feel.

They're not trying to deceive. They're trying to survive the drop.

The crash also creates shame.

People feel weak for needing attention. They feel embarrassed for caring. They judge themselves for not being able to detach.

So they hide it. They pretend they're unbothered. They post as if nothing changed. They maintain the image while privately unraveling.

This is the loneliest part of the cycle.

Being visible while feeling unseen by yourself.

The applause fades, but the expectation remains.

The audience may have moved on, but the person is still waiting for a reaction. That waiting becomes heavy.

Silence starts to feel accusatory. *Why are you not performing? Why are you slowing down? Why are you not giving us what you used to?*

These questions may not be spoken aloud, but they are felt.

And because the attention economy doesn't reward rest, slowing down feels like giving up.

People push harder.

They post more frequently. They force output. They chase trends they do not respect. They compromise boundaries they once held.

Not because they lost values. Because the crash destabilized their sense of self.

When attention fades, people confront something they have been avoiding.

Who am I without the applause? That question is terrifying if you haven't been cultivating an internal identity.

Many people reach this moment and realize they have nothing to fall back on. No quiet sense of worth. No internal validation. No grounded place to land.

Just noise.

This is why the crash can lead to depression.

Not because attention is gone. Because meaning was never built underneath it.

The applause covered emptiness. It didn't resolve it.

When the noise fades, the emptiness gets louder.

This is where some people quit abruptly. They disappear dramatically. They announce breaks that they do not understand. They burn bridges. They sabotage relationships.

They want to escape the pressure. But pressure is not the root problem. Dependency is.

Others double down. They become louder. Sharper. More extreme. They escalate behavior to recapture reaction.

This can work temporarily.

But each escalation makes the eventual crash harder. Because the body adapts again. Tolerance increases. And the baseline rises.

This is how people get trapped in cycles of extreme behavior followed by emotional collapse.

High engagement. Low stability. Over and over.

The crash is not a failure. It's information.

It reveals what attention was doing for you.

It shows you where identity was externalized. Where regulation was outsourced. Where self-worth was built on reaction instead of alignment.

This chapter matters because it names the moment many people experience but do not understand.

The moment when attention stops feeling rewarding and starts feeling necessary.

The moment when applause no longer feels like affirmation becomes survival.

This is where the cost becomes undeniable.

Not publicly. Internally.

Because no one else can feel the crash for you.

They only see the numbers. They do not see the anxiety. The emptiness. The fear of silence.

This is where many people think they're broken. They are not. They're waking up.

Waking up to the realization that attention cannot carry what identity is supposed to hold.

That realization is painful.

But it is also the beginning of something else.

Because once the crash exposes the dependency, there is an opportunity to rebuild.

Not the image. The self.

That's why the next section matters. Because this is where the book turns. Away from exposure. And toward responsibility.

Not shame. But honesty.

The applause fades. And what remains is the truth.

That attention was never meant to be a foundation. It was meant to be a byproduct.

And now that the noise has quieted, the real work can finally begin.

15 | Social Media Did Not Change You, It Revealed You

This is the moment people usually resist.

Not because it is harsh.

But because it removes the last comfortable excuse.

Social media did not change you. It revealed you.

That sentence feels threatening if you're still protecting a narrative. It feels unfair if you believe the platform pulled something out of you that never existed. It feels heavy if you're not ready to own what showed up.

But revelation is not condemnation. It's exposure.

Exposure shows what was already there when pressure arrived. It reveals patterns, not accidents. It brings unconscious behavior into visibility. And once something is visible, it can no longer be explained away.

This is where accountability begins. Not with blame. Not with shame. With honesty.

People often say they have became someone else online. That social media made them louder, harsher, messier, and more reactive. But tools do not invent behavior. They remove constraints.

When the constraints disappeared, something surfaced. That something may not represent who you want to be, but it represents where you were ungrounded.

That distinction matters. Being revealed doesn't mean being defined forever. It means seeing clearly for the first time.

Social media accelerated feedback. It amplified the reaction. It rewarded speed over reflection. Under those conditions, character showed up unfiltered.

What you posted under pressure. How you reacted when challenged. What you chose when attention was on the line.

Those were not glitches. They were data. And data is useful.

This chapter is not about judging that data. It's about reading it honestly.

If you became louder, ask why the quiet didn't feel safe. If you became angrier, ask what you were protecting. If you overshared, ask what you were trying to regulate. If you performed morality, ask what you were afraid to examine internally.

These questions are uncomfortable. But discomfort is the cost of growth.

Accountability without shame means removing the emotional theater around responsibility. It means stopping the performance of guilt and starting the practice of ownership.

Ownership doesn't sound dramatic. It sounds simple.

I did that. I chose that. That behavior came from me. Not from the app. Not from the algorithm. Not from the audience. From me.

This is not a self-attack.

It is self-respect.

Because blaming the platform keeps you powerless. Taking ownership of your behavior gives you agency back.

Agency is the only thing that allows change. As long as social media is the villain, you're the victim. And victims do not choose. They react. They survive. They repeat.

This book is not interested in survival. It's interested in responsibility.

Responsibility doesn't mean you're bad. It means you're capable.

Capable of noticing patterns. Capable of setting boundaries. Capable of choosing differently.

But you can't choose differently if you keep pretending you were forced.

Many people avoid this chapter because it threatens their self-image. They want to believe they're above influence. That they were manipulated. Those circumstances turned them into someone they're not.

Influence is real. Manipulation exists. But influence does not erase choice. It tests it.

Pressure does not create character. It reveals where character is unfinished.

That's not an insult. That's an opportunity.

People who grow the most are not the ones who avoid exposure. They're the ones who let exposure teach them.

Instead of saying *That was not me* they ask *What part of me showed up there?*

That question changes everything. It moves the focus inward, stops the cycle of projection, and interrupts blame.

It also hurts. Because seeing yourself clearly always does. But clarity is what ends cycles. Without it, people keep repeating patterns under new circumstances. New platforms. New audiences. Same behavior.

Social media did not make you perform. It showed you how much you relied on performance. It did not make you angry. It showed you what you do when you feel threatened. It did not make you overshare. It showed you how you regulate pain. It did not make you chase validation. It showed you where self-worth was unfinished.

That revelation is not punishment. It's instruction. And instruction is only useful if you accept it.

Radical responsibility does not mean taking blame for things that are not yours. It means taking ownership of what is.

Your reactions. Your choices. Your boundaries.

This is where people often get defensive. They want to explain, to contextualize, to justify.

Justification delays growth. Not because context doesn't matter, but because explanation can become avoidance.

You don't need to explain yourself to grow. You need to observe yourself honestly.

This is the turning point of the book because this is where the reader stops being a spectator and becomes a participant.

Up until now, the chapters exposed systems, patterns, and incentives. This chapter exposes agency.

Not in a harsh way. In a grounding way.

Because once you stop blaming the system for who you became inside it, you can start deciding who you want to be outside it.

That decision doesn't require an announcement. It doesn't require a post. It doesn't require an audience. It requires honesty.

And honesty is quiet. It happens when no one's watching.

This is where people realize that the most important work will never trend. That growth doesn't come with applause. That rebuilding identity is not content.

It's practice. Social media did not change you. It revealed that you were unfinished.

And being unfinished is not failure. It's permission.

Permission to stop performing. Permission to stop explaining. Permission to start choosing.

This chapter does not end with a solution because solutions come after responsibility.

First comes the mirror.

And if you can look into it without flinching, everything that follows becomes possible. That's the wake-up.

Not shame. Not guilt.

Responsibility.

And responsibility is freedom.

16 | Being Seen Without Being Consumed

Visibility is not the problem. Needing it is.

There is a difference between sharing and relying. Between expression and exposure. Between being seen and being consumed by the need to be seen. Most people never pause to separate the two.

Because the internet deliberately blurs that line.

Being seen feels validating. It feels affirming. It feels like connection. And for people who spent years feeling invisible, visibility can feel like healing.

But healing that depends on reaction is unstable.

This chapter is not about disappearing. It's about containment.

You can be visible without bleeding. You can share without exposing. You can create without erasing yourself.

The mistake many people make after waking up is swinging too far in the opposite direction. They think the answer is silence. Withdrawal. Disappearance.

That is another form of reaction.

This book is not anti-visibility. It is anti-consumption.

Being consumed happens when your worth is tied to response. When your nervous system depends on engagement. When you cannot tell where the content ends, and you begin.

Healthy visibility has boundaries.

Boundaries are not walls. They're filters.

They decide what stays private. They decide what gets processed offline. They decide what doesn't need witnesses.

Most people never learned how to set these because boundaries don't perform. They're quiet. They're internal. They don't announce themselves.

But boundaries are what protect identity.

Without them, visibility becomes invasive.

People begin sharing in real time instead of after reflection. They process publicly instead of privately. They invite the audience into moments that should have been contained.

That is how being seen turns into being consumed.

Healthy visibility asks a different set of questions.

Why am I sharing this? What do I want from this? Would I still share this if no one reacted?

These questions are uncomfortable because they expose motive.

If the answer is relief, pause. If the answer is regulation, stop. If the answer is reaction, reconsider.

Posting with intention doesn't mean posting less. It means posting from alignment instead of urgency.

It means letting moments settle before sharing them. Letting emotions cool. Letting meaning form.

When everything is posted immediately, nothing is integrated.

Integration requires time.

And time is what the attention economy discourages.

This is why many people feel hollow even when they are visible. They are constantly sharing but rarely digesting. They are expressing but not processing.

Healthy visibility respects timing.

Some things are meant to be shared later. Some things are meant to be shared with fewer people. Some things are meant to stay internal.

Not because they're shameful. Because they're sacred.

Sacred things lose power when consumed too quickly.

This chapter is about reclaiming authorship over your exposure.

Instead of asking what will land, you ask what aligns. Instead of asking what will get a reaction, you ask what reflects who you actually are.

That shift is subtle but powerful.

When you post with boundaries, the audience adjusts.

Some will leave. Some will disengage. Some will get confused.

That's not failure. That's filtration.

People who were only there for access will drift. People who were only there for drama will disappear. People who were there for the performance will lose interest.

What remains is smaller but steadier.

And steadiness matters.

Because steadiness supports identity.

Being seen without being consumed requires tolerating less reaction.

That is the hardest part.

When you stop performing, the applause quiets. When you stop exposing, engagement softens. When you stop feeding urgency, attention thins.

This is where people panic.

They mistake quiet for loss.

But quiet is not absence. It's space.

Space to listen to yourself again. Space to notice how you feel without feedback. Space to remember who you are when nothing is being mirrored back.

That space is uncomfortable at first.

Because it reveals how dependent you were.

But dependency is not fixed by more attention.

It's fixed by building internal grounding.

This is where intention becomes essential.

Posting with intention means you are no longer using content to regulate emotion. You are using it to express meaning. You are not asking the audience to hold you. You are offering something you have already held yourself.

That distinction changes everything. People can feel it.

They respond differently. They engage more thoughtfully. Or they don't engage at all.

Both are acceptable. Because your worth is no longer waiting on them.

Being seen without being consumed also means protecting the parts of you that are still becoming.

Growth needs privacy.

You cannot evolve then constantly being watched. You cannot experiment safely while performing for an audience. You cannot make mistakes publicly without them becoming labels.

Some seasons require silence.

Not forever. Just long enough to stabilize.

This is not quitting. It's containment.

Containment allows identity to solidify without pressure. It allows values to deepen without performance. It allows healing to occur without commentary.

And when you return to visibility from that place, the energy is different.

You're not asking to be held. You're offering something whole.

This chapter matters because it shows that the solution is not disappearing or oversharing. It's discernment.

Knowing what to share. Knowing when to share. Knowing why you share.

When those three align, visibility becomes sustainable.

You stop bleeding publicly. You stop chasing reaction. You stop needing applause.

You're still seen. But you're not consumed by it.

And that balance is rare. Because it requires tolerating discomfort long enough for identity to stabilize.

Most people avoid that discomfort. They rush back into the noise.

This chapter invites you to sit in it.

Not to punish yourself. But to reclaim yourself.

Being seen is not the enemy. Being consumed is.

And once you learn the difference, visibility becomes a choice instead of a compulsion.

That is the beginning of freedom. And it leads directly to the next question.

Who are you when no one is watching?

Because until you can answer that honestly, no amount of visibility will ever feel like enough.

17 | Who Are You Without Witnesses

Most people do not know how to answer that question.

Not because they are dishonest.

Because they have not had to.

For a long time, witnesses were optional. Identity was built in private moments. In routines no one clapped for. In decisions that did not get documented. You knew who you were because you lived with yourself when no one else was watching.

That changed.

Now, almost everything can be observed. Recorded. Shared. Reacted to. And when witnessing becomes constant, it starts shaping behavior even when the camera is off.

People begin living as if they're always being watched. They narrate their lives internally. They imagine how moments would look online. They evaluate experiences based on shareability.

This does something subtle.

It replaces self-reference with audience reference.

Instead of asking *Does this feel right to me?* people ask, *How would this look?* Instead of choosing based on values, they choose based on optics.

Identity starts leaning outward. This chapter asks you to pull it back.

Who are you without witnesses? Not the version that performs well. Not the version that explains itself. Not the version that gets validated. The version that exists when there's no one to impress.

That version is often quieter. Slower. Less dramatic. It doesn't announce itself. It doesn't need reaction. And because it doesn't perform, many people neglect it.

They invest in the public self and starve the private one. But the private self is where discipline lives.

Discipline doesn't trend. Purpose doesn't post itself. Consistency happens in silence.

This is why people feel scattered even when they're visible. Their energy is spread outward. They're maintaining an image instead of building a life.

Being alone without witnesses exposes this imbalance.

At first, silence feels uncomfortable. Restlessness sets in. The urge to check the phone appears. The mind searches for stimulation.

This is not boredom. It's withdrawal from constant feedback.

Once the noise settles, something else appears.

Clarity.

People start noticing what they actually enjoy, what drains them, what feels aligned. They notice how often they were performing instead of choosing.

This is where real identity begins forming. Not as a brand. Not as a persona. As a practice.

Who you are without witnesses is defined by what you do when nothing is rewarded.

Do you still read? Do you still reflect? Do you still follow through? Or do things only exist when they can be seen?

This is not a moral judgment. It's a diagnostic.

If nothing feels meaningful without an audience, the audience has become the source of meaning.

That is unstable.

Identity needs roots. Roots grow underground. They do not get likes. They do not get comments. They do not get applause. But they hold everything up.

This is where discipline matters.

Discipline is not about productivity. It's about reliability. About showing up for yourself when no one else is involved. About honoring commitments that don't produce immediate reward.

Discipline builds self-trust. And self-trust is what replaces the need for constant validation.

When you trust yourself, you don't need to be watched to feel real.

Purpose also lives here.

Purpose is not what you tell people you care about. It's what you keep returning to even when it's inconvenient. Even when it's boring. Even when it's unseen.

Purpose is revealed in patterns, not announcements.

People often confuse purpose with passion. Passion is loud. Purpose is steady. Passion burns hot and fast. Purpose sustains.

Social media rewards passion. Life requires purpose.

When people lose touch with who they are without witnesses, they confuse momentum with meaning. They stay busy but feel unfulfilled. They stay visible but feel hollow.

This is why silence feels threatening.

Silence removes the mirror.

Without the mirror, people have to look inward. And if they have not been nurturing the internal self, that reflection can feel empty.

But emptiness is not failure. It's feedback.

It shows you where attention replaced identity.

This chapter is not asking you to disappear. It's asking you to practice being unobserved.

To spend time doing things that will never be posted. To invest energy in relationships that do not generate content. To build routines that exist only for you.

That's how identity stabilizes. That's how self-respect forms.

Attention feels powerful, but respect feels grounding.

Respect comes from living in alignment when no one is watching.

When you know who you are privately, public reaction loses power. Engagement becomes information instead of validation. Criticism becomes feedback instead of a threat.

You can be seen without being shaken.

This is where the internal anchor forms.

And once that anchor is in place, visibility stops being dangerous.

Because it is no longer carrying the weight of your identity.

It is simply expression.

This chapter matters because it reminds the reader of something most people have forgotten.

You existed before the audience.

You mattered before the metrics.

You were someone even when no one knew your name.

Returning to that self is not regression. It's recovery. Recovery of agency. Recovery of clarity. Recovery of choice.

Who you are without witnesses is who you actually are. Everything else is performance. And performance cannot hold you forever.

You need to start rebuilding from the inside out.

Not with announcements.

With practice.

And once that foundation is in place, the final question becomes clear.

How do you use social media without needing it?

18 | Using Social Media Instead of Needing It

Needing something changes your relationship to it.

When you need social media, it controls you. Your mood rises and falls with response. Your sense of relevance depends on engagement. Your silence feels risky. Your presence feels required.

When you use social media, the power shifts back.

This s not about quitting. It's about reclaiming agency.

Social media becomes dangerous when it stops being a tool and starts becoming oxygen. Tools are optional. Oxygen is not. And once something feels essential to your emotional regulation, you are no longer choosing it.

You are responding to it.

Using social media instead of needing it begins with recognizing motive.

Why am I opening this app right now? What am I looking for? What do I expect it to give me?

If the answer is relief, pause. If the answer is validation, pause. If the answer is distraction from discomfort, pause.

Pausing does not mean judging yourself. It means interrupting automatic behavior.

Automatic behavior is where dependency lives.

Most people don't consciously decide to scroll. They reach for the phone reflexively. In quiet moments. In uncomfortable moments. In moments where nothing is happening.

Those moments used to be where thinking occurred. Now they're filled instantly.

Using social media intentionally means letting some silence exist again. It means tolerating boredom without immediately anesthetizing it. It means allowing discomfort to be felt long enough to understand it.

Discomfort is information. It tells you what you've been avoiding. What you've been outsourcing. What you've been numbing.

When social media is used as a tool, it has boundaries. It has purpose. It has timing. It has limits.

You post because you have something to express, not because you need confirmation. You engage because you're curious, not because you are restless. You log off because you're done, not because you are depleted.

That distinction is subtle. But it changes everything.

Using social media requires internal grounding.

You need a sense of self that exists independently of reaction. A place inside you that feels steady, whether a post performs or disappears.

That steadiness doesn't come from confidence. It comes from alignment.

When you are aligned, feedback becomes data instead of identity. Engagement becomes information instead of worth. Criticism becomes input instead of a threat.

You can listen without collapsing.

This is why people who are grounded seem unbothered online. It's not because they don't care. It's because nothing external is carrying their self-image.

They know who they are before they post.

This chapter is not about rigid rules: no posting limits, no detox challenges, no moral performance.

Those things create control, not freedom. Freedom comes from internal clarity.

When you know why you're posting, you don't need to post as often. When you know who you are, you don't need constant reflection. When you have meaning offline, online reaction loses urgency.

Content becomes expression, not compensation. This is the shift.

Creating without self-erasure means you don't trade pieces of yourself for attention. You don't share things you haven't processed. You don't expose wounds for reaction. You don't stay in conflict because it performs.

You choose what you're willing to give. And you keep the rest.

Redfine success online.

Success is not growth at any cost. Success is not constant visibility. Success is not staying relevant forever. Success is sustainability.

Being able to create without burning out, being able to share without bleeding, being able to log off without anxiety.

That is success.

Detaching self-worth from metrics does not mean ignoring metrics. It means understanding their role.

Metrics measure reach. They do not measure meaning. Metrics show reaction. They do not show impact.

Metrics fluctuate based on variables you don't control. Building your worth on them guarantees instability.

When metrics rise, you feel inflated. When they drop, you feel diminished. That cycle never settles.

Using social media means letting metrics inform strategy, not identity.

You can adjust without internalizing. You can respond without reshaping yourself. You can grow without losing grounding.

This requires restraint.

Restraint doesn't trend.

Restraint looks like posting less when you feel compelled to post more. It looks like not responding immediately. It looks like letting moments pass without documentation.

Restraint protects identity.

The goal is not to eliminate desire for attention. The goal is to make attention optional.

Optional things don't control you.

When social media becomes optional, you stop negotiating with it emotionally. You stop measuring your days by engagement. You stop equating visibility with existence.

You use it when it serves you. And you leave when it doesn't.

Freedom is not found in deleting apps or disappearing forever. Freedom is found in sovereignty.

Being able to choose. Being able to pause. Being able to walk away without panic.

That sovereignty comes from internal grounding built in the chapters before this one.

Without that foundation, any attempt to use social media will eventually slide back into need.

But with it, social media becomes what it was always meant to be.

A tool. Not a mirror. Not a regulator. Not an identity.

Just a place where expression can happen without costing you yourself.

This is the final step before this book closes.

Because once you stop needing attention to feel real, you are ready to confront the last truth.

Attention is not love.

And no amount of reaction will ever replace the quiet work of respecting yourself.

That is where this book ends.

19 | Attention Is Not Love

Attention feels close to love.

That is why so many people confuse the two.

Both involve being seen. Both involve response. Both create a feeling of connection.

But attention and love are not the same thing.

Attention is reactive. Love is intentional. Attention shows up quickly. Love stays.

Attention responds to what is loud, urgent, or stimulating.

Love responds to what is real, consistent, and human.

The danger is not that attention exists.

The danger is that attention has been mistaken for something it can never be.

Love.

No amount of likes has ever healed anyone. No amount of views has ever stabilized a nervous system. No amount of applause has ever replaced self-respect.

Attention can distract from pain. It cannot resolve it. Attention can soothe temporarily. It cannot sustain.

And yet, many people build their lives around it as if it could.

They measure their worth by reaction. They measure their days by engagement. They measure their value by visibility.

And when attention fades, they feel unloved.

But attention fading is not rejection. It's reality reasserting itself.

Love doesn't disappear because the room got quieter. Attention does.

Love is not interested in performance. It doesn't require updates. It doesn't need proof.

Love exists even when no one is watching.

That is why attention can feel intoxicating and still leave people empty. Because it mimics the surface of love without offering the substance.

Love requires presence. Attention only requires notice. Love requires commitment. Attention requires reaction.

Love asks something of you.

Attention asks something from you.

This book is not saying attention is evil. Attention can amplify. It can connect. It can introduce. It can open doors.

But attention is not nourishment. And when people try to feed themselves on it, they stay hungry.

This is why silence feels scary to so many people. Because silence removes the illusion. It forces people to confront what attention was covering.

Without attention, some people realize they don't feel loved by themselves. They don't feel grounded. They don't feel whole.

That's not a failure. It's information.

Silence doesn't mean you're losing. It means the noise is no longer buffering you from yourself.

And that is where truth lives.

Love is built in places attention cannot reach.

In discipline practiced without witnesses. In boundaries held without applause. In values honored when it would be easier to perform.

Love shows up as self-respect. Self-respect doesn't trend. It doesn't spike. It doesn't refresh. It doesn't demand reaction.

But it stabilizes.

When you respect yourself, attention loses its power to define you. You can receive it without needing it. You can lose it without collapsing.

You stop negotiating your identity for reaction. You stop confusing being watched with being valued.

This is the quiet shift the book has been pointing toward all along.

Not becoming invisible. Becoming internally anchored.

Attention will come and go. It always has. It always will. Trends change. Audiences move. Algorithms shift.

But self-respect remains.

When you have that, silence stops feeling like failure. It starts feeling like space.

Space to think. Space to choose. Space to become.

This is why the book doesn't end with advice. Advice assumes something is wrong with you. Nothing is wrong with you.

You were just taught to look in the wrong place for what you needed.

Attention felt like love because it was the closest thing available, because it arrived when something inside you was unmet, because it responded when you needed reassurance.

But now you know the difference.

And once you know it, you cannot unknown it.

You can still create. You can still share. You can still be seen.

But you no longer ask attention to carry what it was never meant to hold.

You stop asking it to prove your worth.

You stop asking it to regulate your emotions.

You stop asking it to replace connection with yourself.

That's not withdrawal. That's maturity.

This book ends here because endings don't need applause. They need clarity.

Attention is not love. Reaction is not connection. Visibility is not worth. Silence doesn't mean you failed. It means you're finally listening.

And what you hear there matters more than anything the audience could ever give you.

Because love doesn't shout. It doesn't trend. It doesn't need witnesses.

It waits quietly for you to choose yourself without needing anyone to notice.

That choice will never go viral.

But it will change your life.

And that is enough.

About the Author

WALLO267 is proof that purpose has no borders. After serving twenty years behind bars, he turned his story into a global movement of resilience and reinvention. A *New York Times* bestselling author, cultural advisor at YouTube, former Chief Marketing Officer of Reform Alliance, and co-host of *Million Dollaz Worth of Game* (named by *The Hollywood Reporter* among the most powerful voices in podcasting, 2024), WALLO267 continues to merge impact and innovation. He uses partnerships, like his $4.5 million minority business initiative with Barstool Sports, his lifestyle brand ARPLNSNHOTLS, and his production company Nanny's House Entertainment, which develops and produces movies, TV series, books, and podcasts, to prove your past is data, not destiny.

Keep in Touch with Wallo267

Stay connected, stay inspired, and keep growing with me. I share daily messages, lessons, and moments to help you stay focused on becoming your best self.

Follow & connect on social:

Instagram • Facebook • TikTok • YouTube • X (Twitter)
@WALLO267

For speaking engagements, partnerships,
and media inquiries:

✉ info@wallo267.co,

🌐 www.wallo267.co

Your journey matters.
Keep showing up for yourself every day.